The
Jeffersons

by
Cass R. Sandak

CRESTWOOD HOUSE
New York

Maxwell Macmillan Canada
Toronto

Maxwell Macmillan International
New York Oxford Singapore Sydney

Library of Congress Cataloging-in-Publication Data
Sandak, Cass R.
  The Jeffersons / by Cass R. Sandak.
    p. cm. — (First families)
  Includes bibliographical references and index.
  Summary: An account of the life of Thomas Jefferson and his family, describing his private and political affairs
and the events of his presidency.
  ISBN 0-89686-637-8
    1. Jefferson, Thomas, 1743-1826—Juvenile literature. 2. Jefferson family—Juvenile literature. 3. Presidents—
United States—Biography—Juvenile literature. 4. United States. Declaration of Independence—Juvenile literature.
5. Louisiana Purchase—Juvenile literature. [1. Jefferson, Thomas, 1743-1826. 2. Jefferson family. 3. Presidents.] I.
Title. II. Series: Sandak, Cass R. First families.
  E332.79.S25   1992
  973.4'6'0924—dc20
  [B]   91-33061
                                                                                                         CIP
                                                                                                         AC

Photo Credits
All photos courtesy of The Bettmann Archive.

Macmillan Publishing Company   Maxwell Macmillan Canada, Inc.
866 Third Avenue   1200 Eglinton Avenue East
New York, NY 10022   Suite 200
                                      Don Mills, Ontario M3C 3N1

CRESTWOOD HOUSE

Macmillan Publishing Company is part of the Maxwell Communication Group of Companies.

Produced by Flying Fish Studio

Printed in the United States of America

First edition

10 9 8 7 6 5 4 3 2 1

Contents

Portrait of Thomas Jefferson

4

The Great Declaration

For 17 days in the hot Philadelphia summer of 1776, a delegate to the Second Continental Congress worked busily. The 33-year-old from Virginia was Thomas Jefferson. In Jefferson's time Philadelphia was the most cosmopolitan city in America. It was larger and more prosperous even than Boston or New York. It was also the center of government.

In Philadelphia Jefferson was delighted with his exposure to urban life at its best. The city had paved streets. At night many of them were lighted by whale-oil lamps. The city had libraries and newspapers. Philadelphia even had a college, founded by Benjamin Franklin.

Jefferson worked hard in the second-floor parlor of a three-story brick house on Market Street. But during this time away from home, Jefferson sorely missed his wife. She remained with their daughter at their plantation in Virginia. Jefferson was especially concerned because his beloved Martha suffered from delicate health.

Thomas Jefferson was known as a skilled writer, so he was asked to write down the colonists' grievances against the British. This document, which became the Declaration of Independence, was important because it set forth the reasons why the colonists wanted to break away from Britain. It was an essay that justified setting up a new country made up of the 13 colonies. These colonies would become the first states of the United States of America.

The leaders of the colonial government agreed upon the wording of the declaration on July 2. But it wasn't approved by convention delegates from 12 of the 13 colonies until two days later. Thus, July 4 became the birthdate of the new country.

The declaration was first published a few days later in a Philadelphia newspaper. But only the text of the document appeared. There were no signatures printed along with the text because it was important to keep the identity of the signers secret. In the British view, any signers would be traitors. They would all face death for treason if anyone knew who they were.

The declaration made Thomas Jefferson one of the leaders of his age. After George Washington and Benjamin Franklin, he was the most famous national figure of early America. Many men would be capable of being president. But only a genius such as Thomas Jefferson could create a statement like the Declaration of Independence—one of the world's most significant political documents.

Thomas Jefferson drafting the Declaration of Independence

Young Thomas

Jefferson's ancestors came from Great Britain. The family traced its roots back to the area of Mount Snowdon in Wales. Peter Jefferson, Thomas's father, was tall, broad and immensely strong. He was a Virginia planter and surveyor. The older Jefferson was a hardworking and ambitious man who turned his modest income into a considerable fortune. The family was well-off enough that they could afford a plantation, called Shadwell. The Jefferson home was a big wooden house on the grounds of the estate, about five miles from Charlottesville, Virginia. It was at Shadwell that Thomas Jefferson was born on April 13, 1743.

Thomas's mother, Jane Randolph, was a member of one of Virginia's most distinguished families. Her father, Isham Randolph, was a very wealthy man. She and Peter Jefferson were married in 1739. Thomas had two older sisters. There were also five younger children who came after Thomas.

From his father, Thomas inherited a strong constitution and some 5,000 acres of prime Virginia farmland. From his mother and her Randolph relations, Thomas Jefferson was heir to a privileged position in Virginia society. In those days Virginia was the largest colony. It included not only the area of the present-day state of Virginia, but even lands that would become West Virginia, Ohio, Kentucky, Illinois, Indiana, Wisconsin and Michigan.

Thomas Jefferson was raised at Shadwell until he was almost three. Then the family moved to Tuckahoe, about 50 miles away. Tuckahoe was the estate of William Randolph, who had died. Randolph was a cousin of

Thomas's mother. In his will Randolph had appointed Jefferson's parents guardians of his son and three daughters. They were to raise the children at Tuckahoe until the son, Thomas Mann Randolph, came of age.

One of Jefferson's earliest childhood memories was that of being lifted onto his father's horse for the long ride to Tuckahoe. Young Thomas stayed at the estate until he was about nine. Then the family returned to their Shadwell home.

When Thomas Jefferson was nine, he was sent to live and study with the Reverend William Douglas. This Scottish clergyman ran a boarding school in Northam, Virginia. It was during this period that young Jefferson first studied classical Greek and Latin. Education was very important to the formation of Jefferson's intellect and character.

At first Thomas was not a very eager scholar. He was primarily interested in the out-of-doors. He enjoyed hiking and tramping through the local woods. He loved to hunt for deer and turkeys with his father. Young Thomas also enjoyed music and played the violin. He became a skilled musician.

Peter Jefferson died in 1757 when Thomas was just 14. As the eldest son Thomas might have expected to receive the bulk of his father's estate. But, according to his father's will, Jefferson and his brother were to choose the lands they preferred from among the family's estates.

Thomas's father had wanted his son to continue his education, so Thomas went to a school near Shadwell. It was at this school, run by the Reverend James Maury, that

Famous portrait of Thomas Jefferson painted by C. W. Peale

Thomas really began to enjoy learning. The school was 14 miles from Shadwell, and Thomas stayed at school during the week. He rode home to Shadwell to spend Saturdays and Sundays with his family.

Jefferson entered the College of William and Mary, in Williamsburg, Virginia, when he was 16. At this time, the college was Virginia's only institution of higher learning. It had been founded in 1693 under royal charter and was one of the first colleges in Britain's American colonies.

At William and Mary, Jefferson studied calculus, physics and Greek. During his first year there, he was a careless and indifferent student. But he soon recognized the importance of learning. After applying himself to his work, Jefferson proved himself to be a brilliant student. Because of his knowledge of mathematics and astronomy, Jefferson could calculate when eclipses of the sun or moon would take place.

After two years at William and Mary, Jefferson decided to study law. He was 19 years old. Today students go to law schools to learn the law. In colonial times, there were no such schools. Instead, law students learned by working for lawyers in their offices and watching all aspects of the profession. From 1762 to 1767 Jefferson worked in the Williamsburg law office of George Wythe.

The year that Britain's Parliament passed the Stamp Act—1765—was an eventful year in Jefferson's life. His father had died eight years before. But now that Jefferson was of age, he came into full possession of his many acres of land. He also became a parish vestryman of his church and a justice of the peace. These were positions that reinforced his standing in society.

In May 1766 Jefferson set out on a "grand tour" of American cities. This journey was to serve as a finishing touch on his education. It was the first time Thomas had left Virginia. His travels took him to Annapolis, Maryland, and to Philadelphia and New York. Because of the difficulty his horse and carriage had on the trip, Jefferson sailed home! His trusted black servant Jupiter accompanied him.

Monticello, the house that Jefferson designed and built

After he was admitted to the Virginia bar in 1767, Jefferson practiced law for about seven years on his own in Virginia. Often people lacked ready cash to pay Jefferson for his services. Sometimes they gave him land or animals in exchange for his legal advice. In 1768 Jefferson was elected to the Virginia House of Burgesses. This group was the legislative body of the colony.

The pride of Jefferson's life was the house he designed and built near Shadwell. The house is designed in the Italian classical style. Jefferson called the house Monticello, which is Italian for "little mountain." Jefferson had loved the spot and hoped to build a home there since he first discovered it during his boyhood wanderings. He began the work of clearing the land and starting construction in 1767. The house became a necessity when Shadwell burned to the ground in 1770. In the fire many family heirlooms were lost. Jefferson also lost his books, notes and music.

The Happy Couple

By the time he was a young man, Jefferson stood about six feet two inches tall. His build was sinewy and angular, and he had broad shoulders. His hair was red, and like many redheads, he had freckles. His eyes were gray and reflected his lively intellect. But no one considered him handsome according to the standards of his time. Drawings and portraits reveal a sensitive and kindly face that some might even consider feminine in the delicacy of its features.

Jefferson paid little attention to fashion, except during his courtship days. He did, however, follow the general dress code of his class and of the period. Most of the time he wore a long, dark coat, usually blue. In summer his coat would be made of silk. A waistcoat or vest over a simple white shirt tied with a ruffled stock (in place of a modern necktie), knee breeches and shoes with metal buckles completed the outfit.

This was probably what Thomas Jefferson looked like when he met Martha Wayles Skelton in Williamsburg, around 1770. The daughter of John Wayles, she was a young widow with a baby son. After her husband's death the young mother and her infant son returned to her father's house. She also had a large estate, although it was burdened with heavy debts.

Born in October 1748, Martha was five years younger than Thomas Jefferson. She came from a good family. Her father, John Wayles, was a successful lawyer. No portraits of Martha survive. But from contemporary descriptions of her, we know that she was small and pretty. She had a glowing complexion, auburn hair and hazel eyes. She was warmhearted and kind, though it was said that she had a fiery temper. She was lively and fun, but had a serious side as well. She was better read and educated than most women of her time and social class.

Both Jefferson and Martha Skelton were talented musicians. Martha played the harpsichord and Thomas played the violin. It seems that they were first attracted to each other because of their musical interests.

Before his marriage, Thomas Jefferson had already had one strong emotional attachment. When he was 19, he met a prominent local girl named Rebecca Burwell. She was only 16. Thomas was infatuated with her and spent several months mooning over her. She forms the subject of a number of letters that Jefferson wrote to his friends. In his letters he often called her by a nickname so that no one would know who she really was. Whenever Thomas tried to tell her of his feelings, he became shy and tongue-tied. Eventually, Rebecca met an older and wealthier man and married him instead of Thomas.

Jefferson married Martha Wayles Skelton on New Year's Day in 1772 at The Forest. This was Martha's father's estate. The wedding festivities lasted for several days. The Jeffersons stayed at The Forest until January 18 before starting for Monticello, about 100 miles away.

After riding hard through near-blizzard conditions, the newlyweds arrived at the estate hungry and half frozen on the night of January 26. To make matters worse, the servants had all gone to their own quarters, thinking the couple would not arrive until the next day.

The only part of the house that was ready was a small brick cottage that was 18 feet square. Its single room served as kitchen, parlor and study. This tiny one-room cottage had been Jefferson's bachelor quarters before his marriage. There was no food in the house and only a half bottle of wine.

It was a romantic beginning for their life together. For the next three months they stayed alone at Monticello. They saw only their servants and guests, who steered their horses up the rough mountain track to visit the newlyweds.

The Jeffersons had five of their own children, but only two daughters survived infancy. The first of these was born in September 1772. Her name was Martha, but as a young girl she was known as Patsy. In the beginning she was a sickly child, and for the first few months it was thought she might die. But a nurse took good care of her, and she seemed to recover and grow strong. Patsy was always the daughter closest to her father.

Her younger sister's name was Mary, but she was called Polly while she was growing up and Maria when she was older. It is said that Jefferson's younger daughter strongly resembled her mother in her pale and delicate beauty.

Martha's son by her first husband died in 1773. Certainly these infant deaths were sad events. But in colonial times, parents expected that children might die and were somehow better prepared to deal with these losses.

Events Leading to War

It was during the early years of the Jefferson marriage that the American colonies began protesting English domination. In Virginia's House of Burgesses, Jefferson had plenty of opportunities to suggest a number of reforms. Some of these were local improvements, but some also involved issues on a larger scale. And all the while, Jefferson was gaining political experience.

In 1775 Jefferson traveled back and forth to Philadelphia several times. By this time the colonies were already in revolt. He was now a member of the Second Continental Congress. At 32 he was also its youngest member. This group was called together to set up a unified governing body for the colonies.

In 1776 Jefferson and other members of the Congress met in Philadelphia. They wanted a written document to declare their independence from England. Jefferson became the primary writer of the Declaration of Independence. To do so, he collected all of his thoughts on the idea of liberty and political philosophy gathered from a lifetime of reading and learning.

Jefferson was never an eloquent public speaker. But he was a brilliant writer. He forged his reputation first in Virginia's House of Burgesses and later in the Continental Congress, not as a fiery orator, but as a deep and serious thinker who could write careful arguments and justifications of his beliefs and opinions. For this reason he was charged with writing the Declaration of Independence.

Other members of the declaration committee were John Adams, Benjamin Franklin, Roger Sherman and Robert Livingston. Adams had worked hard to make Jefferson chairman of the committee, as he was far and away the best writer of the group. And the writing is almost entirely his. Adams made two small changes; Franklin made five. Sherman and Livingston contributed their opinions and assents.

The Revolutionary War was fought from 1775 to 1781. When the war was over, the colonies had won their independence from England. Independence became official with the signing of the Treaty of Paris in 1783.

Thomas Jefferson as chairman of the committee drafting the Declaration of Independence

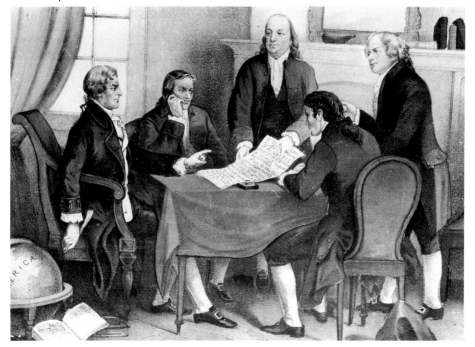

The Death of Martha

The Jeffersons' marriage lasted just over ten years. Jefferson described his marriage as a period of "unchequered happiness." Martha died in September 1782, when she was just 33 years old. She had given birth in May of that year to another daughter, Lucy Elizabeth. A frail woman, Martha never fully regained her strength. And the baby lived only a few months longer than her mother.

Jefferson was plunged into "a stupor that rendered me as dead to the world as she. . . ." It took him almost a year to come out of seclusion. At that time Jefferson sent for his unmarried sister, Anna Scott Jefferson. She came to join the household at Monticello. Jefferson's daughters were still very young when their mother died.

In the month following his wife's death, Jefferson was elected to Congress. He took Patsy to a boarding school in Philadelphia. He left Polly and the baby, Lucy Elizabeth, with his dead wife's half sister, Elizabeth Wayles Eppes, and her husband at their estate in Eppington.

After Martha's death, Jefferson got rid of most of her possessions. He wanted to keep only his memories of her. True to those memories, Jefferson never remarried, although he was still a relatively young man (39) when she died and lived another 42 years. There is a popular story that Martha's hold on Thomas was so strong that on her deathbed she made him promise never to remarry. Many think that Thomas was so in love with Martha that he refused to marry again after her death.

Portrait of Jefferson in France negotiating commercial treaties with European powers

Governor and Ambassador

In June 1779 Jefferson had been appointed governor of Virginia. This was during the war and the position demanded quick military decisions. Jefferson could not hold back the British invasion of Virginia. Jefferson was not a skilled strategist. He had many strengths, but fighting and organizing fighting men were not among them. Jefferson's indecisiveness drew much criticism. However, after an inquiry was made into his actions as governor, he was cleared of any charges of incompetence.

In 1784 a lonely Jefferson went to France. He had just eight weeks to settle his affairs and make all the arrangements for the journey. Jefferson and his elder daughter, Patsy, sailed on July 4, 1784, and arrived in France in August.

Jefferson went to France to negotiate commercial treaties with European powers. From 1785 on, Jefferson served as American ambassador to France, replacing Benjamin Franklin, who was now an old man.

Jefferson remained in France for five years. He liked French things and favored cultivating relations with France. Jefferson thought that friendship with Great Britain would be difficult until the British adjusted to American independence. And, as ambassador, he had a job to do.

While in Paris, Jefferson became infatuated with Maria Cosway. She was the young, attractive wife of a prominent English painter living in the French capital. Maria was also an artist and devoted to music. Jefferson and Maria Cosway had long talks and visited gardens and other places of interest. But there is no evidence that they ever spent time together alone.

It appears that Maria was just a flirt who played with Jefferson's affections for her and did not return his feelings. She slipped away from Paris without saying good-bye to Jefferson, and he regretted the energy and emotion that he had spent on the affair.

Jefferson's daughter Patsy went with her father to France, while her younger sister stayed home for the first few years. At 12, Patsy was impressionable. She was educated at a convent school run by an order of Roman Catholic nuns. She took to her education so well that she eventually wanted to convert to Catholicism and become a nun. Jefferson was so shocked that he removed her from the school. He himself supervised the remainder of her educa-

Jefferson's daughter, Martha (Patsy)

tion in France. Back in the United States, Patsy appeared to have overcome her desire for celibacy. She married her second cousin, Thomas Mann Randolph, and the couple had 12 children.

Polly reluctantly joined her father in France in July 1787. More than two years of coaxing had failed to persuade the girl to leave her relatives and make the ocean crossing. Polly did not want to leave her aunt and uncle and her cousins, the closest family she had ever known. In desperation her aunts lured her to a birthday party on board a ship docked near the Eppes family estate. After hours of games and partying, the exhausted girl fell asleep. When she awoke, the ship had already set sail on the voyage that would take her to her father and sister. Abigail Adams looked after the girl in London for three weeks before Jefferson sent a friend to bring Polly to Paris.

Also in 1787 Jefferson had made a long journey to the south of France and into Italy. He was most impressed by the glories of Roman architecture and resolved to build a dome at Monticello when he returned. He also observed the farming methods of Italy's Piedmont region. He stole grains of Italy's famous rice to bring back home, even though this was a crime punishable by death. Jefferson is credited with having introduced the cultivation of rice in the southern United States.

While Jefferson was in France, the Constitution was being written back in Philadelphia. Jefferson was not present to contribute his ideas. His main criticism of the newly written Constitution was the lack of a list of individual rights. In just a short time, however, the Bill of Rights would correct this.

In the summer of 1789, the French Revolution was just beginning. Jefferson and his daughters closed up their home in Paris and returned to the United States. Jefferson wanted to be part of the new republic.

Appointments and Elections

Soon after Jefferson returned from France in 1789, the country's first president, George Washington, asked him to be a part of the new government as secretary of state.

In that first cabinet there were only four positions. One of the four was secretary of the treasury held by Alexander Hamilton. From the beginning Jefferson and Hamilton disagreed on almost every issue. Jefferson did not believe in too strong a central government; Hamilton did. Jefferson believed in good relations with France; Hamilton felt that Great Britain was the place to cultivate political friendships.

Because Jefferson and Hamilton were so often opposed, two different philosophies of government were being created. In the long run, Jefferson stood for a Republican form of government, while Hamilton represented the Federalist point of view. The Federalist party believed in a strong central government, while the Republican party favored states' rights. It was the beginning of the political party system in the United States.

The differences between Hamilton and Jefferson continued to cause bad feeling within the cabinet. In 1793 Jefferson retired, happy to return to Monticello. But many people wanted Jefferson to become president, and the Virginia planter was soon lured back into politics.

In 1796 Jefferson ran against John Adams for president. He did not win. John Adams, a Federalist, was elected the second president of the United States. In those days, the

*Thomas Jefferson around the
time of the presidential
election of 1800*

runner-up automatically became the vice president, no
matter what party. Jefferson thus became vice president.
Serving in this office helped prepare him for his next job.

Jefferson and Aaron Burr ran on the same ticket in the
presidential election of 1800. They tied, each receiving 73
electoral votes. In those days you just ran for office, without
stating what you were running for. Neither one had made
clear in advance who would be president and who would
be vice president. The vote went to the House of Representatives to decide the winner. But the House voted 35 times,
and each time the result was a tie. Finally, Jefferson's old
enemy, Alexander Hamilton, intervened. He lobbied to
break the tie, which allowed Jefferson to become president.
Somehow he thought Jefferson would be easier to deal with
than Burr. (His instinct would prove correct when a few
years later, Hamilton and Burr dueled, and Hamilton lost.)

Jefferson as President

As head of a large and powerful country—even if it was a new one—the president carried heavy responsibilities. Along with the political duties came the social ones. The president's household was naturally the hub of Washington society. Entertainments involved the leaders of the nation and of Congress. Visiting dignitaries from foreign lands were also expected to be well received.

Jefferson's inauguration, on March 4, 1801, was a simple but dignified affair. It set the tone for his terms in office.

Jefferson was the first president to rely on a first lady who was not his wife. James and Dolley Madison had been living in retirement at their Virginia estate, Montpelier, when Jefferson appointed Madison to his cabinet as secretary of state.

Madison's wife, Dolley, was chosen to serve as Jefferson's official White House hostess. Dolley Madison was well known and well liked as a social figure.

Dolley Madison, Jefferson's official White House hostess

25

At that time, the White House was a large but plain building. The Adamses had been the first presidential family to live there. They had not gone far with decorating and furnishing the president's house. But Jefferson did the best he could. He was alone much of the time, and so he lived in only a small portion of the executive mansion. Still, the home was one of the nicest places in the new nation's capital, for much of Washington, D.C. was still muddy swampland and not very attractive.

Both Adams and Washington had been close to England in spirit. Their lifestyles reflected a "royal" tradition. Jefferson was a plain man and probably the first truly "American" president.

The White House

When the great new city that would become Washington, D.C., was being planned, Thomas Jefferson was President Washington's secretary of state. The architect for the new city was Charles L'Enfant. Many people thought his plans were too grand and too European for the capital city of a democracy. Jefferson was one of these people.

Jefferson also thought of himself as an architect and city planner. In fact, he strongly urged that the capital's buildings be kept to a maximum height of three or four stories. This would keep the skyline clear so that there would always be a sense of light and space. Much of the success and beauty of Washington today is the result of Jefferson's foresight.

It was only natural that Jefferson and L'Enfant would come into conflict. Both men had even submitted their own designs for the president's mansion. They both lost to James Hoban, the Irish-born architect who designed the building that came to be known as the White House.

Thomas Jefferson was only the second president to live in the recently completed White House. As soon as Jefferson moved in, he discovered that the roof leaked. So he commissioned Benjamin Latrobe, a young architect, to repair the White House roof. Latrobe himself was a skilled builder and was working at the time on the Capitol building rising nearby.

Jefferson also saw a chance to impose his own ideas on the Executive Mansion. His renovations made the structure more in keeping with his own original design for the house. Many of these ideas were never carried out. One thing Jefferson did, however, had a lasting effect. He ordered the outside of the building to be whitewashed to keep its stone surface fresh. The Executive Mansion thus became the "White" House, although it would not really be called that for several years to come.

In addition to the leaking roof, Jefferson found that much of the exterior landscaping had not yet been done. He laid out the first lawns and gardens around the house. He also supervised the planting of trees and ornamental shrubs.

During Jefferson's presidency, the first White House wedding took place. Dolley Madison's youngest sister, Mary Payne, married John Jackson, who later became a general in the U.S. Army. The bride was also related to George Washington through one of Washington's brothers.

Although Jefferson did not have his own first lady to

serve as hostess, he still gave elaborate dinners, but in a democratic way. He replaced formal receptions with smaller open houses. Military bands provided tasteful music. Jefferson served good food and fine wines, but he tended to do it informally.

More and more, the atmosphere of a democratic American society—rather than one based on aristocratic European traditions—was being stamped on entertainment at the White House. And in 1801 Jefferson had become the first president to open the mansion to the general public. Succeeding presidents maintained this custom until well into the 20th century. The result, however, was that sometimes the crowds got out of hand.

By the time Jefferson became president in 1801, he had been a widower for more than twenty years. Martha and Thomas Jefferson's two girls remained close to their father, even after they had each married. In fact, Patsy was often at the White House, helping her father with entertaining. But she had her own large family so she found it challenging to combine the roles of mother and hostess.

When Patsy grew up, she wanted to be known by her given name of Martha. In 1790 she married her second cousin, Thomas Mann Randolph, in a ceremony at Monticello. In many respects, Martha was very like her father, while Polly was more like her mother. Polly married her cousin John Wayles Eppes in 1797.

The Jefferson family made its mark on the history of the White House. Jefferson's daughter Martha Randolph gave birth to the first child ever born in the White House. This grandson of Jefferson's was named James Madison Randolph, after the close family friend.

Jefferson's younger daughter Mary (Polly) died in 1804, aged 26. Like her mother, Mary died shortly after giving birth to a child. This upset the 61-year-old president immensely. He then turned his attention to his one surviving daughter and his many grandchildren.

Stories tell us that Thomas Jefferson introduced several popular foods at the White House. Often, he gave these foods to his grandchildren as special treats. From Holland he brought waffles, and from Italy came macaroni. From his visits to France, Jefferson brought almonds and anchovies. But the most popular dish of all was a frozen cream dessert served in a pastry shell. Jefferson brought the recipe from France and it was called ice cream. In this way Thomas Jefferson introduced ice cream to America.

At Christmas of 1805, Jefferson sent for all six of his grandchildren. He and Dolley Madison gave a festive party for more than a hundred children. They threw open the doors of the mansion and welcomed everyone. Guests were served sweet punch and cakes. Jefferson enjoyed himself so much that he played his violin. For several hours everyone was enchanted with the music and good cheer.

A painting of the meeting of representatives during the Louisiana Purchase

The Louisiana Purchase

Without a doubt, the greatest achievement of Jefferson's presidency was the Louisiana Purchase. Napoleon had abandoned his dreams of extending his French empire into the New World, but he needed cash to finance his military exploits in Europe. So he decided to sell the more than 800,000 square miles of the Louisiana Territory. Jefferson was president in 1803 when the United States bought this huge tract of land from France for $15 million. Jefferson sent James Monroe to France to help with the negotiations. Monroe had previously been ambassador to France and was well liked and trusted there. The Louisiana Purchase nearly doubled the size of the United States. It extended the country's borders as far west as the Rocky Mountains. Less than one percent of the territory was settled at the time.

In 1804 Jefferson's government asked two scouts to explore this land. They were Meriwether Lewis and William Clark. Jefferson was delighted two years later when Lewis and Clark returned with exciting stories of their adventures in the rich new land. They brought back souvenirs for Jefferson, which he proudly displayed, first at the White House and then in a permanent collection at Monticello.

Lewis and Clark brought back animal pelts and buffalo robes, Indian headdresses and ceremonial garments. They also brought back a menagerie of wild animals, including a number of grizzly bears that delighted the Jefferson grandchildren. The president decided to share the bears with the nation by making a home for them on the White House lawn. Even after Jefferson's term of office ended, the grounds were still referred to as the "Bear Garden."

Jefferson's Presidential Achievements

In his first term, Jefferson had dealt with the Barbary pirates. This group of bandits preyed on American ships off the north coast of Africa. They demanded increasing amounts of money to allow U.S. ships to sail safely. Jefferson sent vessels and marines to Tripoli to defeat the enemy—successfully. The battle became the first U.S. victory on foreign soil.

Early in his first term, Jefferson also repealed the Alien and Sedition acts. He had denounced both of these when they were made into law and was delighted to be able to see the end of them. He also ended the liquor tax that had brought about the Whiskey Rebellion.

The country was growing and seemed to be flourishing. Jefferson was easily reelected in 1804 and served a second term, beginning with another inauguration in March of 1805. In the 1804 election, voters cast their votes for a vice president for the first time.

During Jefferson's second term, Britain continued to cause trouble on the world's oceans. Jefferson saw the Embargo Act of 1807 as one way to challenge the British. But the plan did not work out at all. Restricting the sale of British goods in North America had a disastrous effect on U.S. commerce. The national economy was more than a little shaky at this point, and Jefferson was blamed for bringing the country near bankruptcy.

Jefferson could probably have run for a third time in 1808. But he was 65 years old and wanted—as always—to get back to Monticello. And so he left Washington for his estate once more.

Monticello

Monticello, the lovely estate he had built near Charlottesville, Virginia, was where Jefferson always found peace. In the intervals between his various positions serving the government, he would return again and again to Monticello.

As president, Jefferson often returned to Monticello, his home in Charlottesville, Virginia.

Jefferson had begun designing the house when he was 24 years old. Among Jefferson's first projects were leveling the hilltop, building a road up the steep hill and constructing a kiln to fire the thousands of bricks that would be needed to construct the house.

By 1772, when Jefferson married, only a small part of the house was ready. Even by the time his wife, Martha, died ten years later, the house was nothing like the one we know today. It took almost 25 years for Jefferson to get the house to its finished condition. Virtually all the materials used came from the estate.

One of the many spacious rooms in Monticello

Jefferson kept revising his plans for the house as his own experiences widened and exposed him to new ideas and influences. Jefferson based his design for the house on the work of the Italian architect, Andrea Palladio. The house itself is formal and symmetrical. It is far more spacious inside than it appears from the outside. From a distance the house looks as if it has only two stories, when it actually has three.

After Jefferson came back from France in 1789, he began to add more rooms and higher ceilings and to build the distinctive dome. The dome at Monticello was the first ever placed on an American house.

Monticello was originally a farm, and Jefferson and his staff grew many kinds of crops. Jefferson took an active interest in the science of agriculture. He experimented with new types of plants and livestock. Crops such as garlic, orange trees and wine grapes were grown for the first time in the United States by Thomas Jefferson at Monticello.

Among Jefferson's most important horticultural achievements was the cultivation of the grapevine in Virginia. Jefferson wrote that "he who introduces a new plant to cultivation does more for the happiness of mankind than any other benefactor."

Monticello has formal parks on its grounds, and the landscaping is neat and precise. There are some 30 separate gardens on the grounds. There are many outbuildings, and underground passageways connect these buildings with each other and with the main building.

Jefferson was also an inventor. He invented a plow and later invented the seven-day calendar clock that is mounted in the main entrance hallway at Monticello. Some of his other inventions are on display in the house. He devised a kind of swivel chair and a tilt-top table that was ideal for artists. Jefferson also perfected a polygraph machine that could make multiple copies of handwritten documents.

After the White House

After he left the White House, Jefferson lived for 17 more years. During his retirement at Monticello, his daughter Martha Randolph and her family also made their home there with him. Jefferson enjoyed good health, but he was not well off. By the time he died, he was heavily in debt. His daughter Martha was eventually forced to sell Monticello to pay these debts.

It was only after serving as president that Jefferson began the work of founding and designing the University of Virginia, at Charlottesville. The property was bought in 1816, but it wasn't until 1819 that the name, the University of Virginia, was chosen. Jefferson had been inspired by Benjamin Franklin's University of Pennsylvania. He wanted Virginia to have another good school besides the College of William and Mary, and one that did not have royal or sectarian associations.

Not only did the 71-year-old Jefferson design the buildings for the campus, but he laid out the grounds and made plans for the curriculum. To top it all off, he served as the first rector of the university.

A mountain view of the University of Virginia, Charlottesville, and Monticello

Even in retirement, Jefferson kept up an active routine. There was a steady stream of visitors, as well as varying numbers of family members, who lived at Monticello for long periods of time. The kitchen servants were always bustling to feed the swarms of guests. Often, there were 20 or more at one time.

Jefferson's daily routine began before dawn with a few hours devoted to correspondence. From breakfast until lunchtime, he inspected the gardens and workshops of the estate. Sometimes he mounted a horse to ride out and oversee the fields and livestock on the several farms that made up the estate. From lunch until evening, the time was devoted to conversation, music or games with neighbors and friends. From early evening until bedtime, he read.

Jefferson's good health continued, and he attributed this to his regular habits and moderation in food and drink. He was firm with his many grandchildren, but none of them recalled ever hearing him "utter a harsh word to one of us, or speak in a raised tone of voice, or use a threat." He set rules for their behavior. "He simply said 'Do' or 'Do not.'"

Toward the end of his life, Jefferson wrote to John Adams. Early in their careers, the two men had been close friends. But they had also had many differences. Although they had shared much, they differed over the political party system. In old age they buried their disagreements and enjoyed a complete reconciliation.

In 1815 Jefferson sold his library of 6,000 books to the government. They founded what would become the Library of Congress. The previous collection of books owned by Congress had been destroyed during the War of 1812. Thomas Jefferson had always been an avid reader and collected books on many subjects.

Jefferson the Man

Jefferson was a lifelong foe of oppression. In a private letter written in the midst of political turmoil, Jefferson confided to a friend: "I have sworn upon the altar of God eternal hostility against every form of tyranny over the mind of man." He fought against intolerance and superstition.

Political caricature of Thomas Jefferson attacking his intellectual and political ideas

Jefferson had been educated by an Anglican clergyman and later at an Anglican college. He had served as a vestryman and remained a member of the Episcopal church throughout his life. However, his beliefs were more liberal (even radical) than those of other church members of his, or even our own, time. He even feared that if the United States were to have an "established" religion such as England's, tied to the government and its leaders, it could lead to widespread discrimination and bigotry.

Jefferson was the author of the Statute on Religious Freedom, which marked an end to the English government's role in Virginia's churches. Jefferson's advanced ideals were born in the intellectual ferment of the European Enlightenment. Thinkers in England, France and other European countries said that the solutions to problems were to be found through the use of human intelligence. They stressed reason, tolerance and liberty.

His personal attitudes on the subject of slavery were extremely enlightened for his time. In the South in the 18th century, slavery was part of the fabric of economic life. Thomas Jefferson kept slaves. But by every report, they were well treated, and many were even considered family members.

There were, interestingly, persistent rumors that Jefferson was intimate with one of his slaves. Her name was Sally Hemings. Some say there were children as a result of this union, but no one has yet proven this to be true. The Hemingses were actually half brothers and half sisters of Jefferson's wife, Martha. After burying his third wife, Martha Wayles's father had taken one of his black slaves as a mistress.

It appears that the stories were concocted by a disgruntled political opponent of Jefferson's. And, in fact, one of Jefferson's nephews made a deathbed confession in which he confessed to having a decades-long affair with Sally. He admitted that he was the father of her children and that his uncle, Thomas Jefferson, was entirely innocent. This seems most probably the case. Jefferson's personality was such that he tended to romanticize and idealize women. He was shy and easily hurt. It does not seem likely that he was a great womanizer.

Jefferson's Legacy

President John F. Kennedy remarked at a dinner that he hosted in November 1962 for a number of Nobel Prize winners that his guests represented "the most extraordinary collection of talents that has ever gathered together at the White House with the possible exception of when Thomas Jefferson dined alone."

Such praise may appear excessive, but it is fully warranted. Thomas Jefferson was a remarkable man. He was a statesman, a philosopher and an architect, in addition to all his other talents.

The list of Jefferson's achievements includes his work as lawyer, inventor, linguist, agronomist, philosopher, essayist, botanist, musician, archaeologist and architect. In addition to Monticello and the buildings at the University of Virginia, Jefferson designed his friend James Monroe's estate, Oak Hill, near Washington, D.C. He also devoted more than four decades of his rich, full life to the service of

Declaration of Independence.

Fac-simile of the original document in the hand-writing of Thomas Jefferson.

[Copied by permission from the MS. in the Department of State, at Washington.]

A Declaration by the Representatives of the UNITED STATES OF AMERICA, in General Congress assembled.

When in the course of human events it becomes necessary for one people to dissolve the political bands which have connected them with another, and to assume among the powers of the earth the separate and equal station to which the laws of nature & of nature's god entitle them, a decent respect to the opinions of mankind requires that they should declare the causes which impel them to the separation.

We hold these truths to be self-evident, that all men are created equal, that they are endowed by their creator with equal & inherent & inalienable rights, that among these are life & liberty, & the pursuit of happiness; that to secure these rights, governments are instituted among men, deriving their just powers from the consent of the governed; that whenever any form of government becomes destructive of these ends, it is the right of the people to alter or to abolish it, & to institute new government, laying it's foundation on such principles & organising it's powers in such form, as to them shall seem most likely to effect their safety & happiness. prudence indeed will dictate that governments long established should not be changed for light & transient causes: and accordingly all experience hath shewn that mankind are more disposed to suffer while evils are sufferable, than to right themselves by abolishing the forms to which they are accustomed but

Copy of the Declaration of Independence in Thomas Jefferson's handwriting

his country through politics. Because of the breadth of his interests and the level of his accomplishments, he has been compared with Leonardo da Vinci.

Jefferson called the presidency "a splendid misery." He dismissed his accomplishments as one of America's greatest statesmen thus: "Nature intended me for the tranquil pursuits of science. . . . [But] the enormities of the times in which I have lived have forced me. . . . to commit myself [to] the boisterous ocean of political passions."

when a long train of abuses & usurpations [begun at a distinguished period
&] pursuing invariably the same object, evinces a design to ~~subject~~ reduce
them under absolute Despotism, it is their right, it is their duty, to throw off such
government & to provide new guards for their future security. such has
been the patient sufferance of these colonies. & such is now the necessity
which constrains them to [expunge] their former systems of government.
the history of the present ~~majesty~~ King of Great Britain, is a history of [unremitting] injuries and
usurpations, [among which appears no solitary fact to contra-
dict the uniform tenor of the rest all of which have in direct object the
establishment of an absolute tyranny over these states. to prove this, let facts be
submitted to a candid world. [for the truth of which we pledge a faith
yet unsullied by falsehood]
he has refused his assent to laws the most wholesome and necessary for the pub-
-lic good:
he has forbidden his governors to pass laws of immediate & pressing importance,
  unless suspended in their operation till his assent should be obtained,
  and when so suspended, he has utterly neglected ~~utterly~~ to attend to them.
he has refused to pass other laws for the accommodation of large districts of people
  unless those people would relinquish the right of representation in the legislature, a right
  inestimable to them, & formidable to tyrants only:
he has called together legislative bodies at places unusual, uncomfortable, & distant from
  the depository of their public records, for the sole purpose of fatiguing them into compliance
  with his measures;
he has dissolved Representative houses repeatedly [& continually] for opposing with
  manly firmness his invasions on the rights of the people:
  ~~and continued~~, he has refused for a long time after such Dissolutions, to cause others to be elected

2

*The
Declaration of
Independence*

On July 4, 1826, Jefferson died. It was the 50th anniversary of the Declaration of Independence. It was also the same day that John Adams died in Massachusetts. They were the only two signers of the Declaration of Independence who had gone on to become presidents of the United States.

Jefferson had indeed been invited to go to Washington for the celebrations. But he was 83 years old and his health was failing. He suffered from rheumatism, and toward the

end, there was most likely a tumor that caused him great discomfort. He knew the great celebration was coming, but he lost consciousness a few days before the Fourth. He had a few lucid moments after that, and he asked anxiously if it was the Fourth of July. He wanted so much to see his country celebrate 50 years of freedom.

In a simple service at Monticello, Jefferson was buried next to his beloved Martha and his daughter Mary. At his request, Jefferson's tombstone contains only the following inscription: "Here was buried Thomas Jefferson, author of the Declaration of American Independence, of the Statute of Virginia for Religious Freedom, and Father of the University of Virginia."

The epitaph modestly makes no mention that the aristocratic Virginian served two terms as president, was also vice president, governor of Virginia, minister to France, secretary of state and member of Congress. But the legacy of Thomas Jefferson lives on through the work that he performed in the cause of freedom and in helping to build the nation we know today.

The gravestone of Thomas Jefferson

For Further Reading

Bober, Natalie S. *Thomas Jefferson, Man on a Mountain*. New York: Atheneum, 1988.

Bruns, Roger. *Thomas Jefferson (World Leaders Past and Present)*. New York: Chelsea House, 1986.

Fisher, Leonard Everett. *The White House*. New York: Holiday House, 1989.

Friedel, Frank. *The Presidents of the United States of America*. Revised edition. Washington, D.C.: The White House Historical Association, 1989.

Hargrave, Jim. *Thomas Jefferson (Encyclopedia of Presidents)*. Chicago: Children's Press, 1986.

Klapthor, Margaret Brown. *The First Ladies*. Revised edition. Washington, D.C.: The White House Historical Association, 1989.

Lindsay, Rae. *The Presidents' First Ladies*. New York: Franklin Watts, 1989.

The Living White House. Revised edition. Washington, D.C.: The White House Historical Association, 1987.

Patterson, Charles. *Thomas Jefferson*. New York: Franklin Watts, 1987.

St. George, Judith. *The White House: Cornerstone of a Nation*. New York: G. P. Putnam's Sons, 1990.

Stefoff, Rebecca. *Thomas Jefferson, 3rd President of the United States*. Ada, Okla.: Garrett Educational Corporation, 1988.

Taylor, Tim. *The Book of Presidents*. New York: Arno Press, 1972.

The White House. Washington, D.C.: The White House Historical Association, 1987.

Index